My New Room

Julie Haydon

Contents

Rigby.

A Harcourt Achieve Imprint

www.Rigby.com
1-800-531-5015

My New Room

This is my new room.

Mom and Dad

look at my plan.

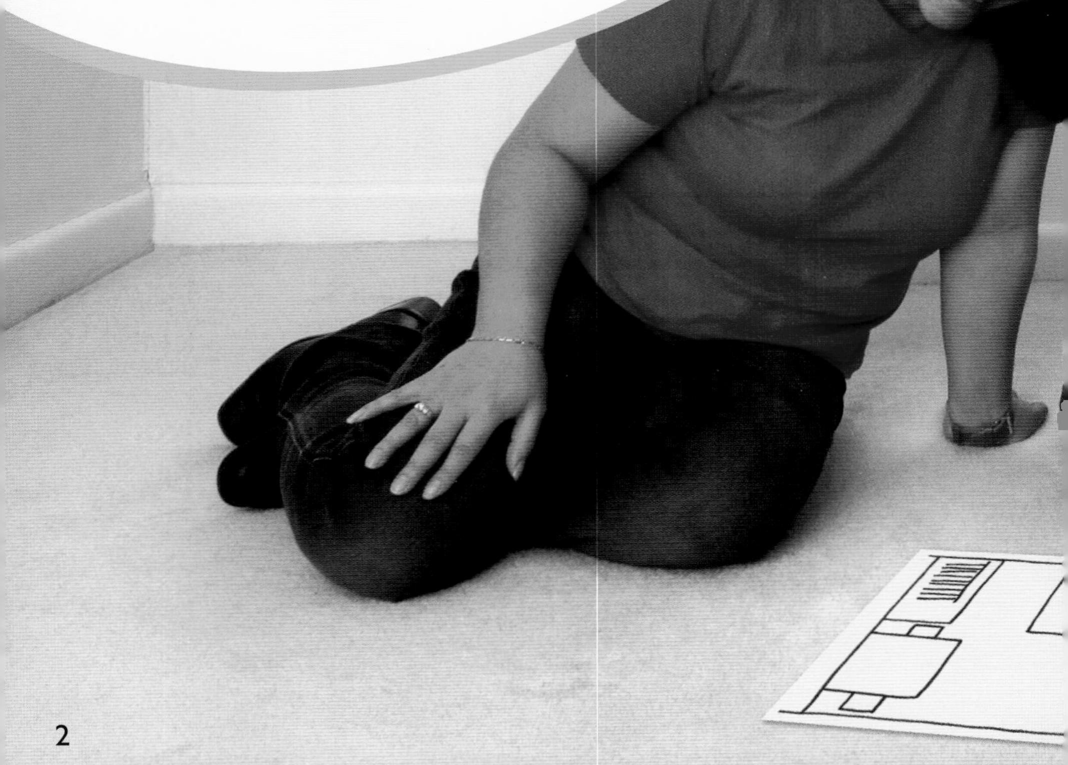

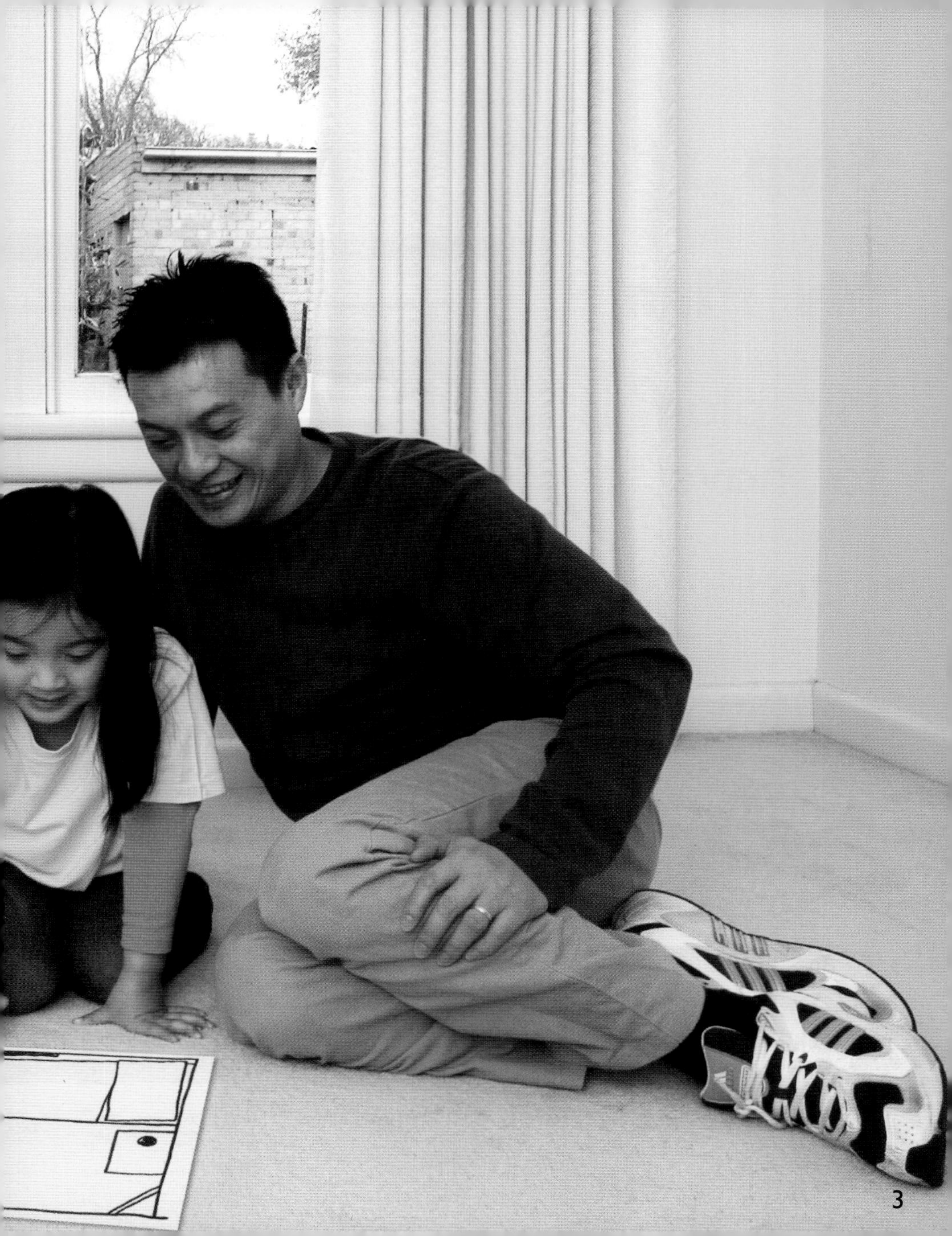

Step 1:

My Plan

My plan is to have a:

- bed
- shelf
- table
- chair
- lamp

shelf
chair
table
chair

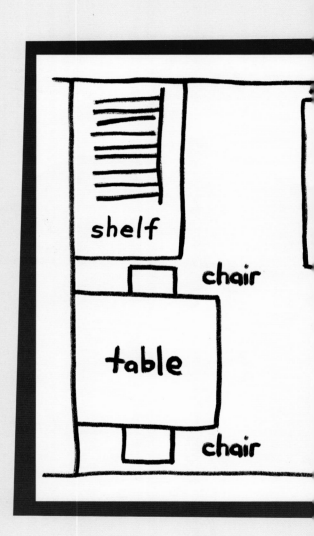

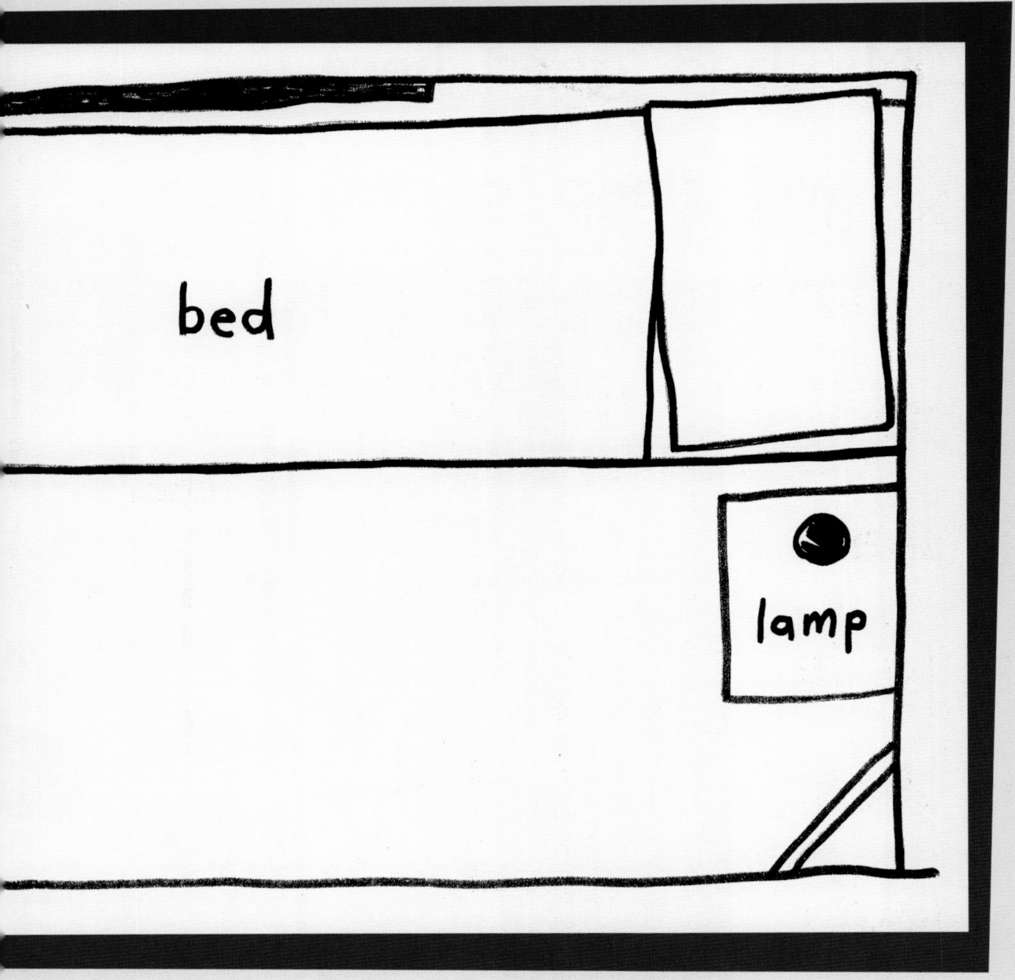
bed
lamp

Step 2: My Bed

My bed goes here.

I will sleep on my bed.

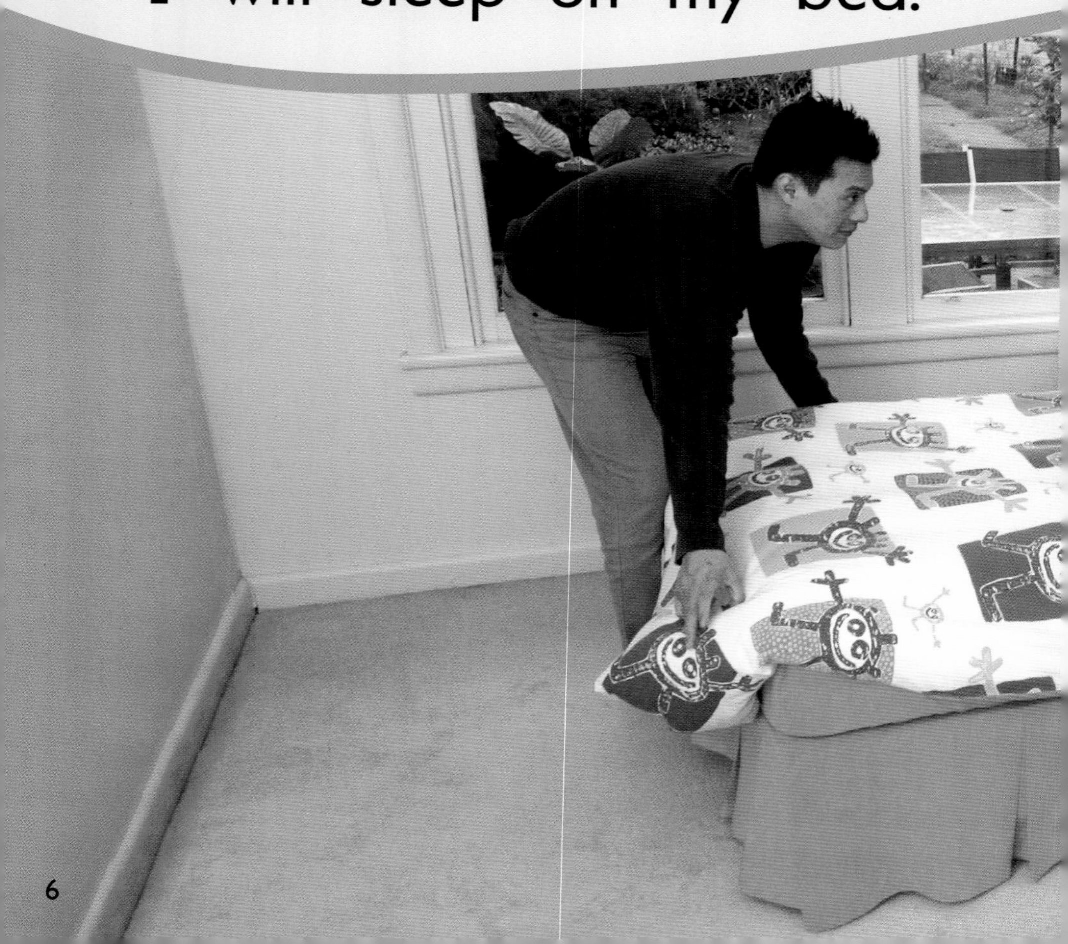

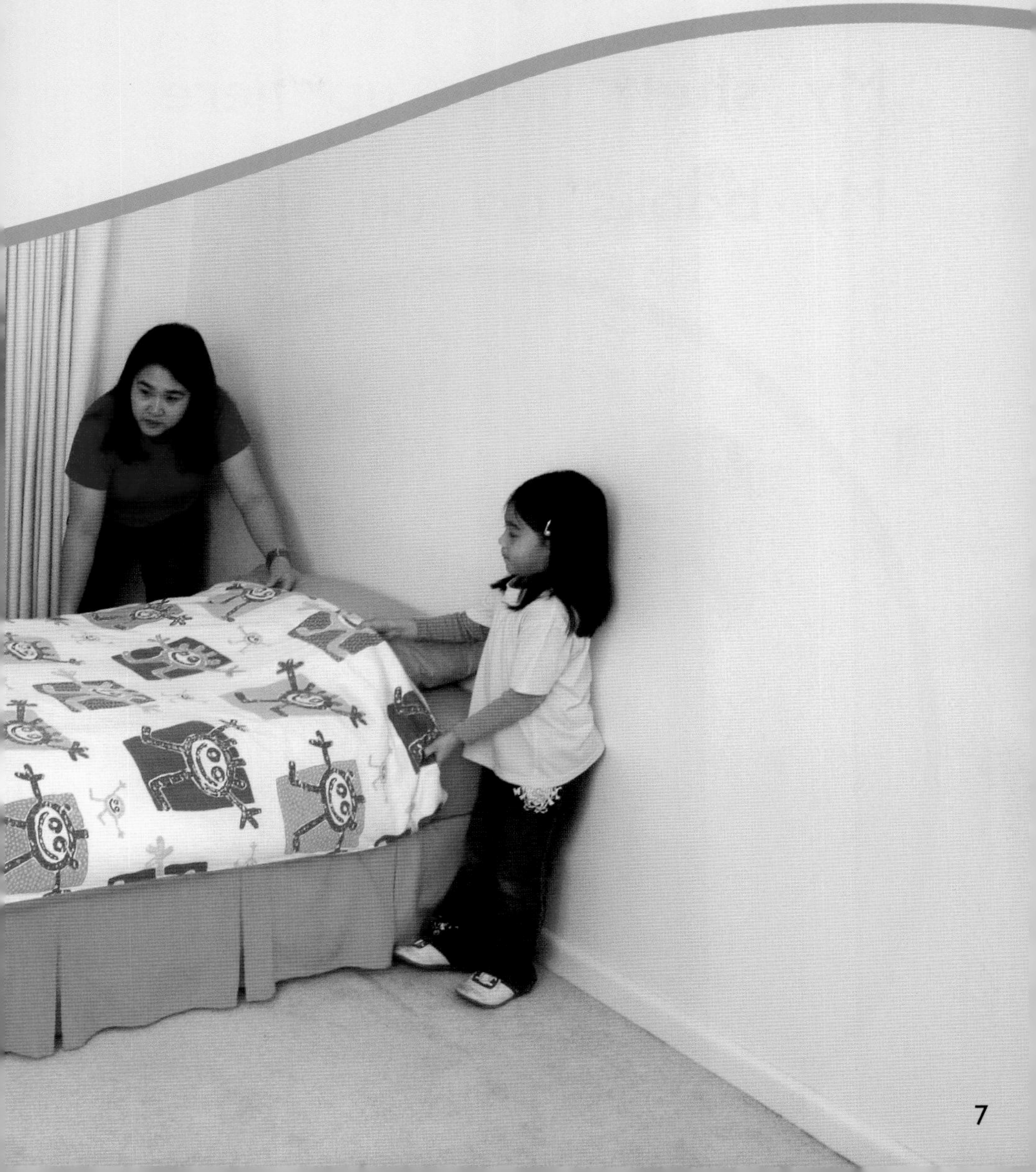

Step 3: My Shelf

My **shelf** goes up here.

My books go on the shelf.

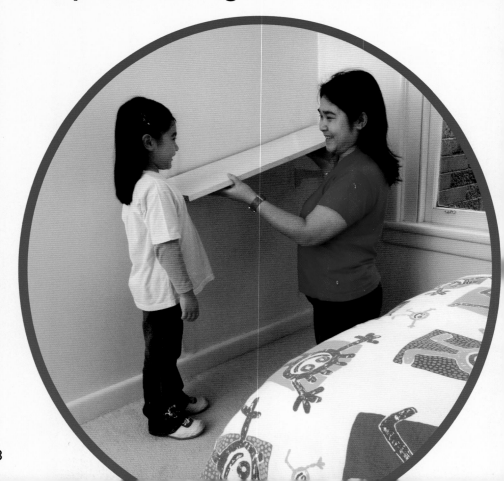

Step 4: My Lamp

My lamp

goes by my bed.

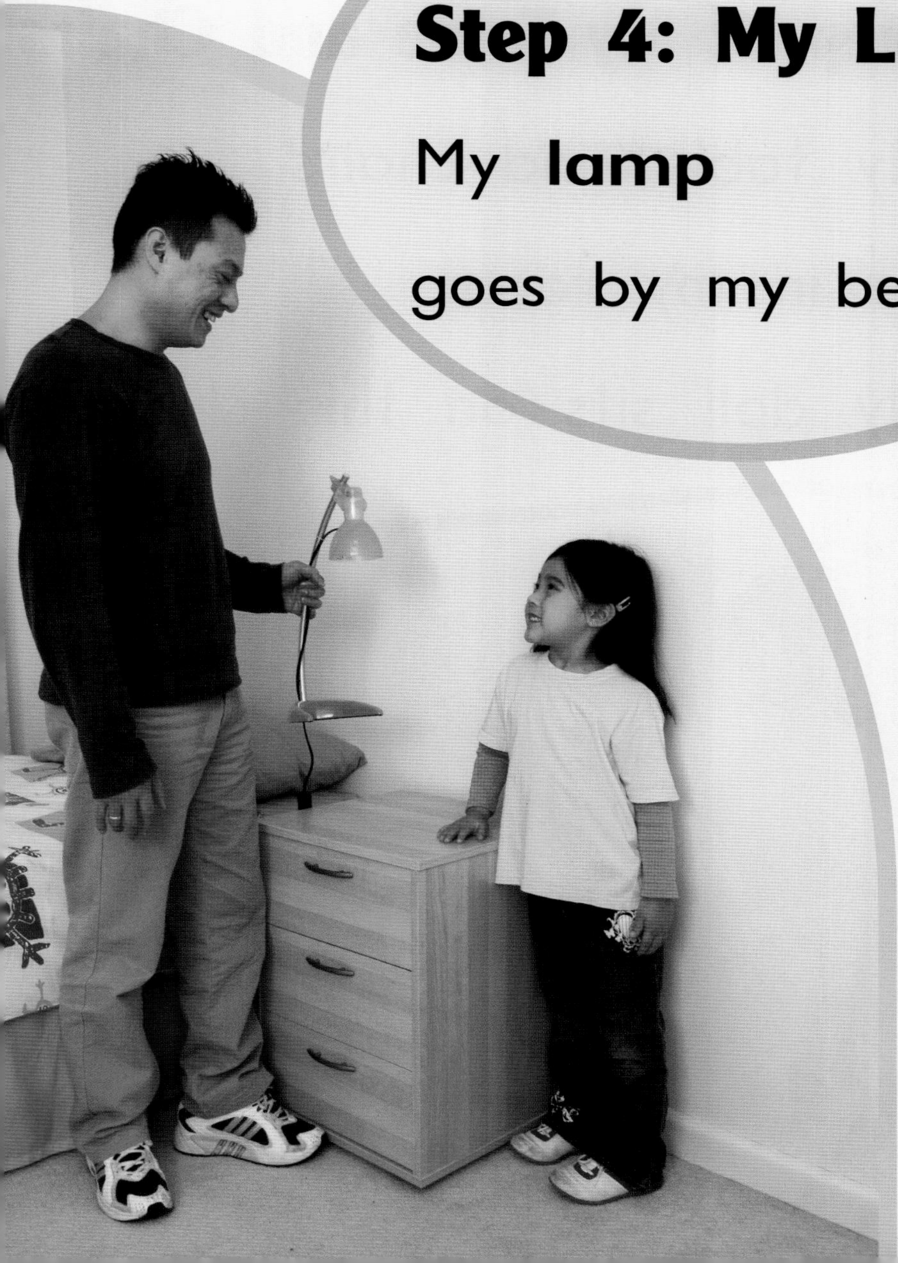

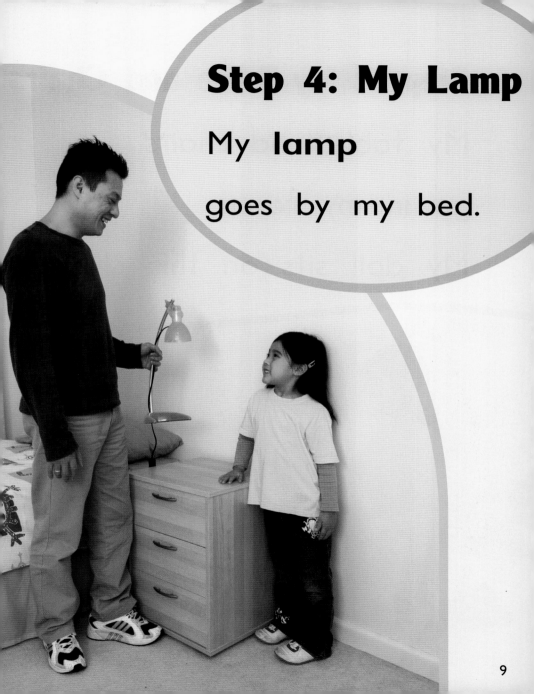

Step 5: My Table and Chairs

My table and chairs

go in my room.

My doll sits on this chair.

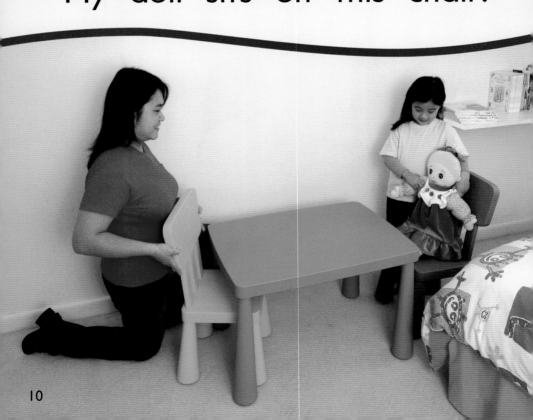

Step 6: My Butterfly

My butterfly
goes on the wall.

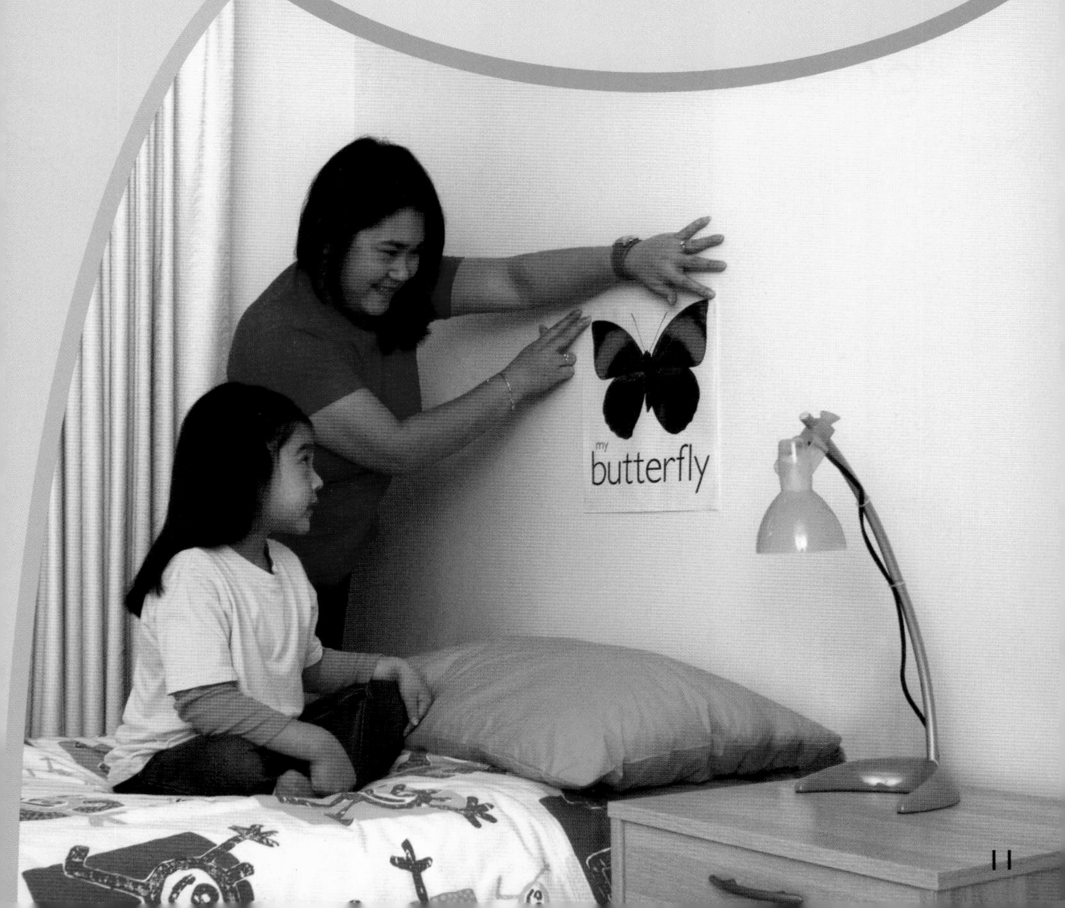
my
butterfly

Step 7: My Toys

My toys are in a box.

My monkey

goes on the shelf.

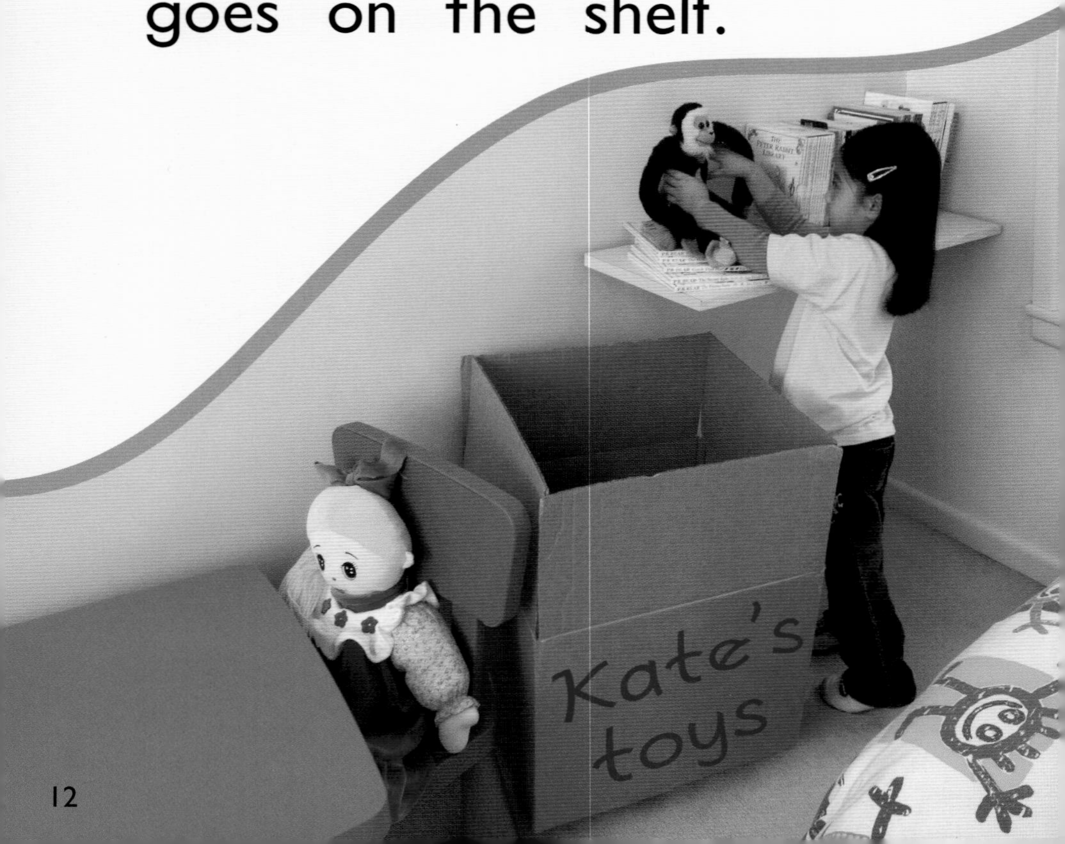
Kate's
toys

My frog goes on my bed.

My ball goes here.

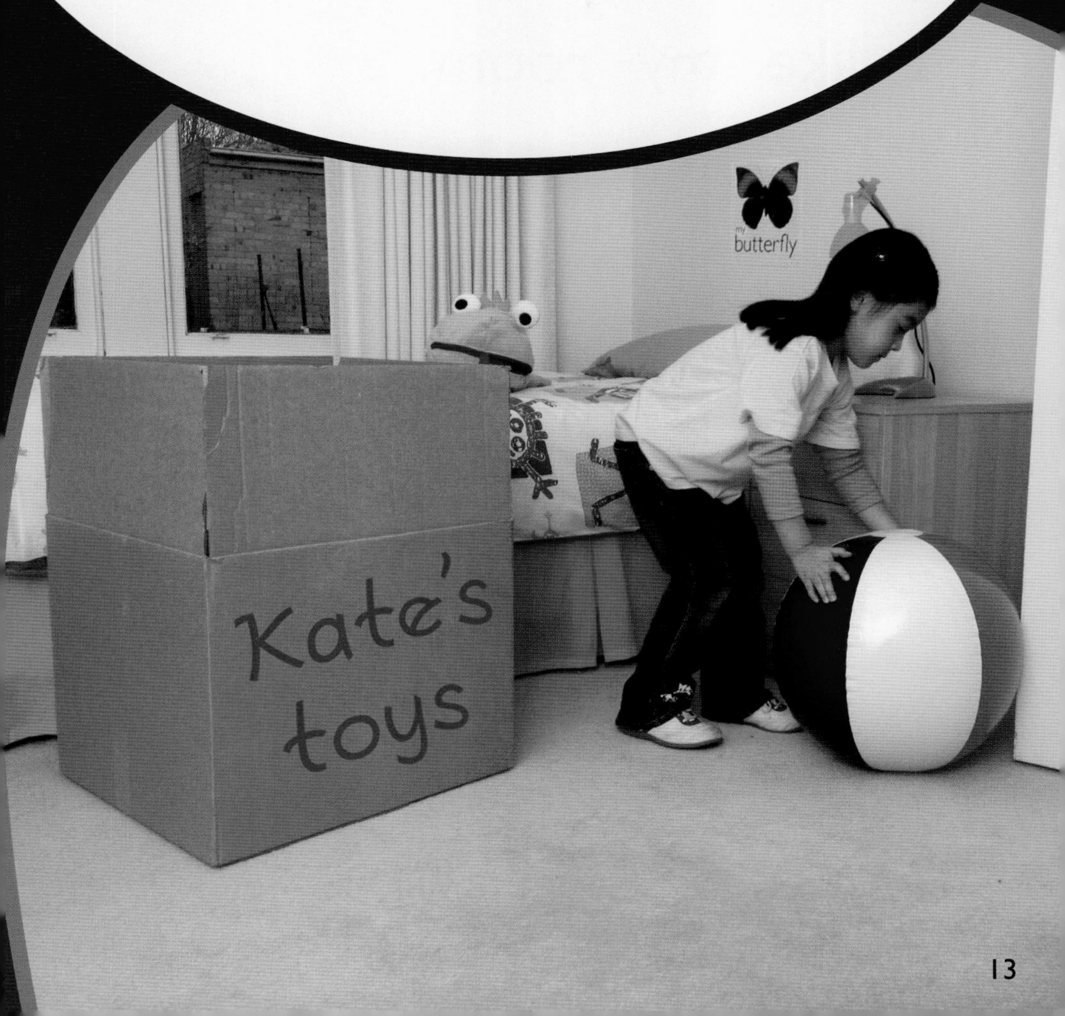
my
butterfly
Kate's
toys

I Like My Room

My new room looks good.

I like my room.

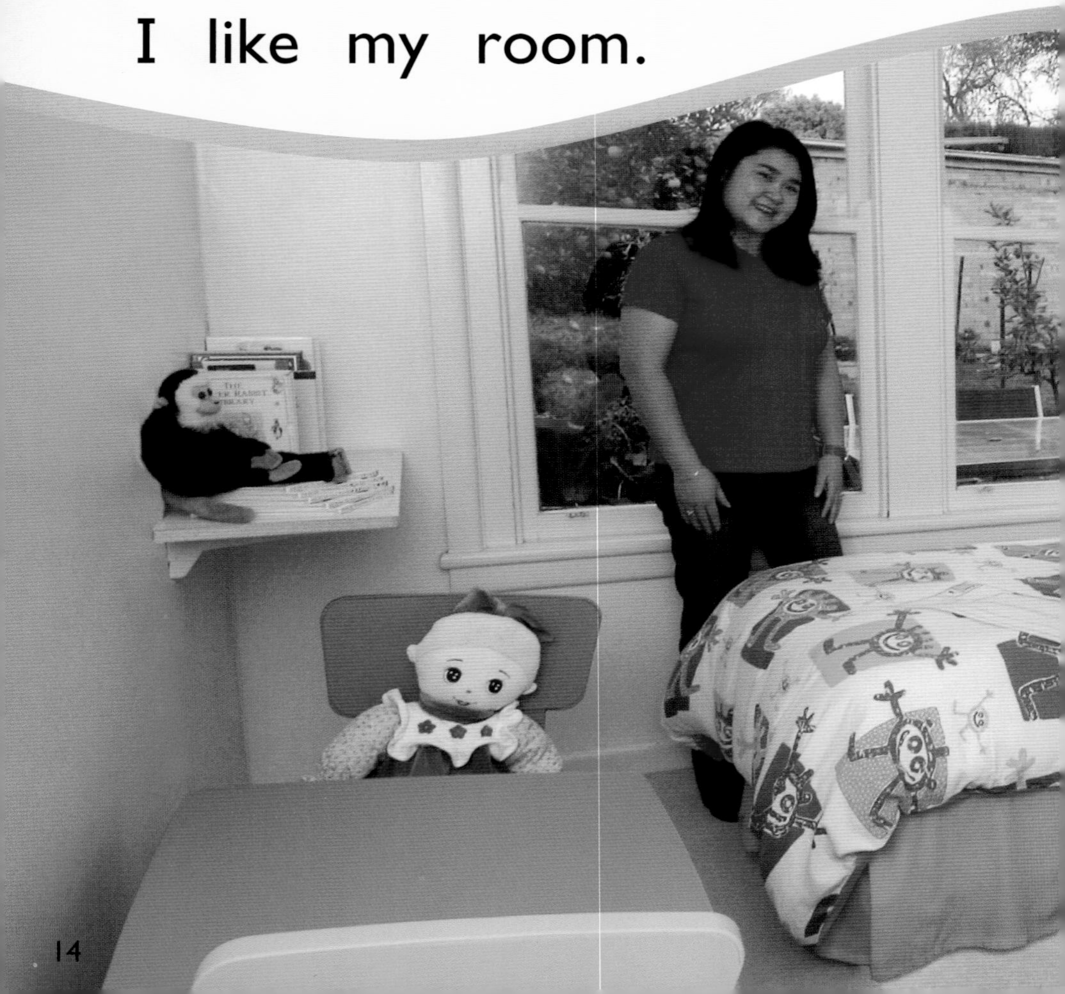

Mom and Dad

like my room, too.

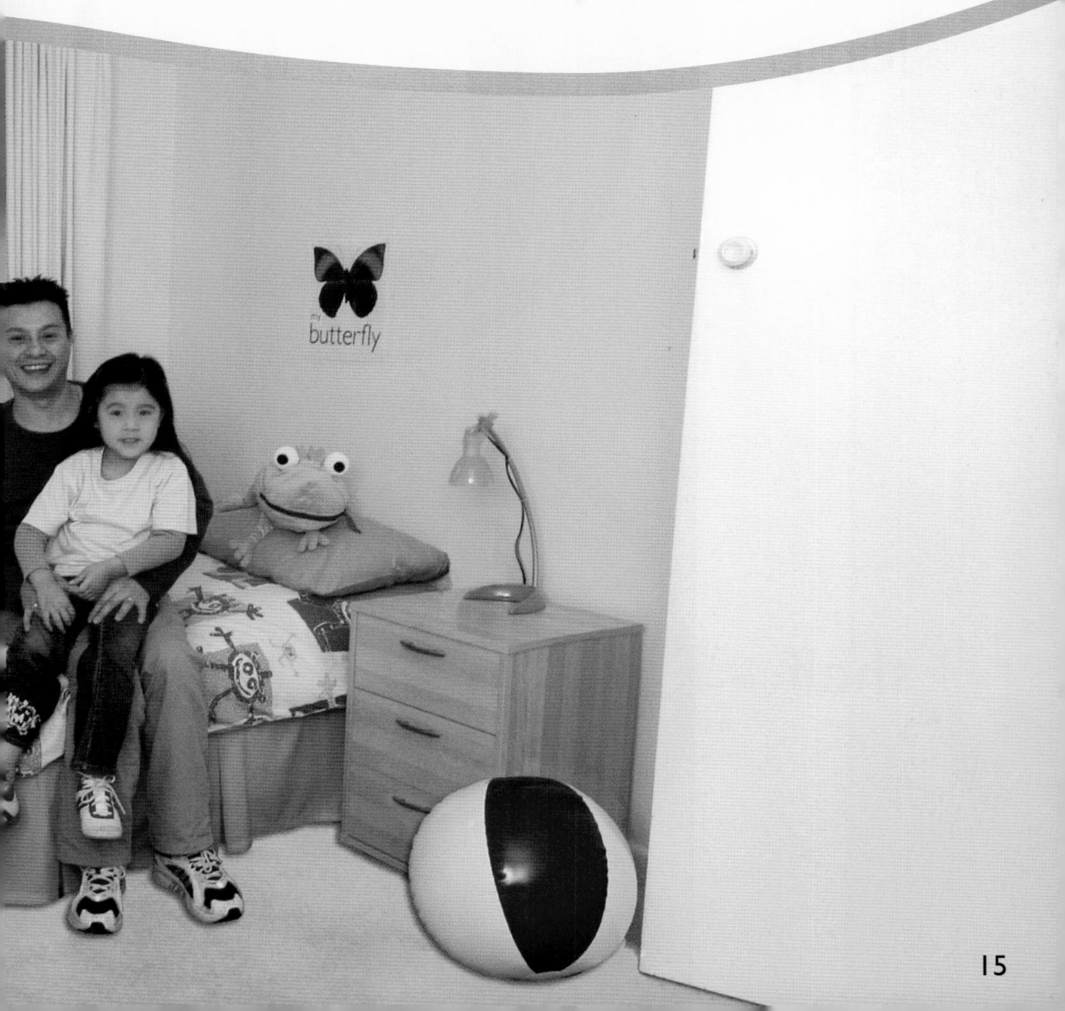
my
butterfly

Glossary

lamp

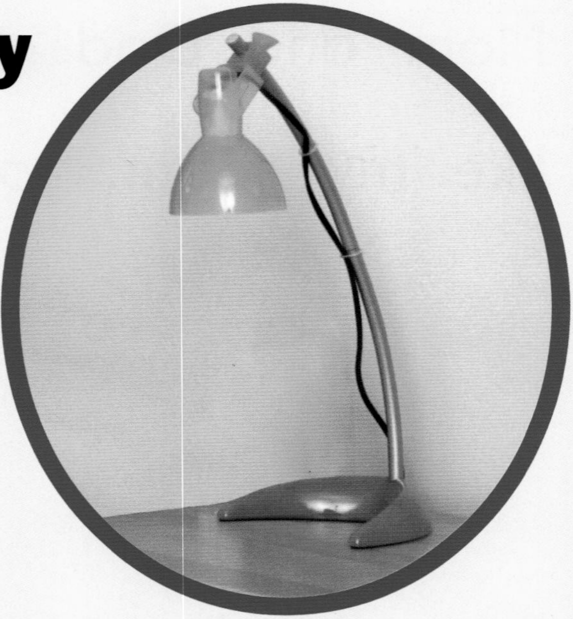

shelf

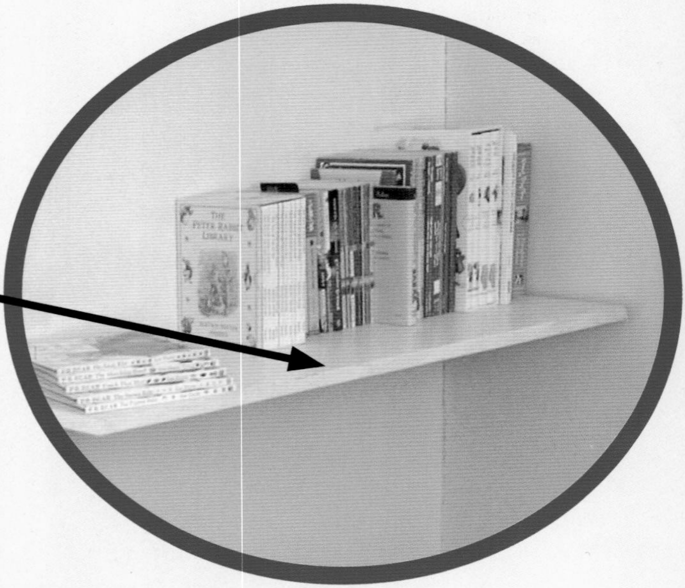
THE PETER RABBIT LIBRARY